LLM
DISSERTATION

HOW TO MAXIMISE MARKS FOR YOUR PRACTICE FOCUSED DISSERTATION

PUBLISHED BY INSPIRED TO STUDY LTD

ALSO BY INSPIRED TO STUDY LTD.

How To Write a 1st Class Essay
10 Reasons You Didn't Write An Outstanding Opinion

All titles available in print and eBook on Amazon &
www.inspiredtostudy.org

SUZANNE REECE

LLM
DISSERTATION

HOW TO MAXIMISE MARKS FOR YOUR PRACTICE FOCUSED DISSERTATION

PUBLISHED BY INSPIRED TO STUDY LTD

First published in Great Britain 2018
By Inspired to Study Ltd
©Copyright Suzanne Reece

Print ISBN: 978-0-9955436-2-1

Electronic ISBN: 978-0-9955436-9-0

DEDICATION

This book is dedicated to the memory of
Mrs Violet Eunice Reece
And
Ms Aretha Franklin
Both
women
taught me courage and joy

CONTENTS

Also by Inspired to Study Ltd.

ii

Dedication

v

Contents

vii

Foreword

xi

Introduction

1

1.

READ YOUR ASSESSMENT CRITERIA AND RULES BEFORE YOU CHOOSE YOUR LAW DISSERTATION

8

2.

FOLLOW YOUR PASSION AND YOU WILL FIND YOUR MOTIVATION

18

3.

CONSIDER ALL REASONS FOR
WRITING YOUR LAW DISSERTATION
28

4.

IDENTIFY THE ISSUES YOUR DISSERTATION
WILL COVER AT AN EARLY STAGE
36

5.

IDENTIFY A THESIS QUESTION WORTHY
OF AN EXCEPTIONAL DISSERTATION
42

6.

TEST IT BEFORE YOU USE IT
50

7.

FORM YOUR OWN OPINIONS AND
DISCUSS THEM IN YOUR DISSERTATION
58

8.

PLANNING, TIMING AND DELIVERY

66

9.

SURVIVAL TIPS

78

APPENDIX A
90

APPENDIX B
92

APPENDIX C
93

APPENDIX D
95

BIBLIOGRAPHY
101

ABOUT THE AUTHOR
103

ACKNOWLEDGMENTS
105

FOREWORD

I first met Suzanne when she taught civil advocacy on the Bar Professional Training Course at City University London. I discovered that she was an experienced tutor with a wealth of experience from legal practice. We kept in touch after I left law school.

I was always keen to hear about Suzanne's latest projects and was pleased to hear that she had finished her third book; *LLM Dissertation: How to Maximise Marks for your Practice Focused Dissertation*. I was even more surprised when she asked me to review the book and write this foreword. The next feeling was one of panic …what did I know about writing a foreword? I am not a famous reviewer, but I can offer you a sincere and honest opinion of the book. I have also had to write two dissertations in my academic life, one for my undergraduate degree and the second for my LLM. I understand the highs and lows of writing your first dissertation and the difference in writing for masters levels.

Reassured that I was equipped for the task I sat down in a comfortable chair and began to read the book. I read the book carefully and thoroughly. The book is specifically written for post-graduate law students but as I read I thought a lot of the advice and tasks are very transferable to other subjects.

My honest opinion is this is an absolute gem of a book. As I read the book it took me back to the days when I had to plan and write my own LLM dissertation. If I had known half of the information and advice Suzanne sets out in this book, the whole process of writing my dissertation would have been lot easier and more enjoyable. Writing a dissertation is a difficult task and it is easy to be overwhelmed by the whole process. This book offers compassion, wisdom and courage to anyone writing a dissertation.

Saddy Njie

September 2018

INTRODUCTION

"The journey of a thousand miles begins with one step."

— LAO TZU, CHINESE PHILOSOPHER

Many law students have an opportunity to complete a dissertation when they "top-up" their post-graduate studies on the LPC or BPTC. This book is specifically aimed at law students who are undertaking this practice-focused law dissertation. Law undergraduates undertaking their first dissertation may also find this book of general use.

If you are undertaking a general dissertation you may find this book helpful but bear in mind the specific requirements of your own subject. If you are undertaking a dissertation for a PhD, then I am sorry this book is not for you and I suggest you put it down.

In this book we will NOT be looking at how you carry out research, referencing or discuss primary and secondary research methods. We will NOT discuss writing your law dissertation. There are many useful university library guides and tools to help you with these topics. We will solely focus on the first difficult steps of selecting your law dissertation topic. This is a task that requires a great deal of attention because if you get this right it is the foundation to your practice-focused law dissertation and the key to maximising your grades.

This task of writing a practice-focused law dissertation for your post-graduate studies will be new. You will not have not done any work that will match the level of detailed research and planning this task will require. The time and energy you will take to complete your law dissertation will exceed any other written work you have done so far.

A law dissertation is a completely different task to writing an extended law essay. An unhelpful definition of a dissertation is: "a long essay especially one written for a university degree". This is a little like comparing shopping for a new pair of jeans with buying your first car! Both activities involve a purchase, but they are of very different magnitudes.

Your law dissertation will require you to master some key tasks and demonstrate core skills. You must:-

- Show that you understand research techniques and methods;

- Demonstrate an understanding of using relevant legislation and caselaw;

- Critically analyse your research results;

- Produce research data that supports your thesis;

- Examine the practical application of your area of law;

- Master writing a new form of academic work;

- And finally SCORE MAXIMUM MARKS on the assessment criteria.

The best part of this assignment is that you have the freedom within the confines of the course programme to choose the subject and topic for your law dissertation. Once you decide on a subject that you find interesting your natural inquisitiveness will take over and you will find the research and writing much easier than writing essays on topics that are set for you by your university. So how do you get from that curious and interested student to someone who produces, after a lot of hard work, an amazing law dissertation?

All students start out intending to get a top grade. For some students somewhere along the path, enthusiasm wanes and the tasks turn into a burden. Some students become overwhelmed by the volume of research and have no clear path or understanding of where their research is leading them. The desire for the top grade disappears and these students just want to get the task done. It is at this stage that the scale of the tasks and looming deadlines can make students focus on the wrong issues. They think more about the word count and throwing everything into their dissertation rather than the quality of their work.

These students end up simply reproducing and repeating their research data without proper evaluation. This is a dangerous path leading you away from evaluation, critical analysis and the confidence to express your own views. This is the path to writing a law dissertation that lacks the essential attributes of an amazing dissertation.

Students often came to my first supervision meeting keen to explain why they wanted to write a law dissertation on their chosen subject. They were passionate about the subject matter and keen to do their best. What I often found was that despite their enthusiasm they had failed to consider some basic preparation for choosing their dissertation topic and failed to decide how they intended to conduct their research.

In this book I will take you through the essential steps to selecting your dissertation topic and working title. You will be better prepared for your literature review and understand what you need to do to achieve that exceptional grade for your law dissertation.

This is a book to help YOU prepare, plan and organise your first practice-focused law dissertation; so I have written it in an easy to follow style. You will need to have your favourite note-taking App open or a new work book. There are exercises for you to complete. Complete the exercises as you read. They are designed to test and help you refine your dissertation topic ideas. I want you to pause, put this book down and spend time just thinking.

The best time to read this book is BEFORE you have chosen your law dissertation topic. If you have already completed this step, then use this book to check that you have not missed out any important steps in your planning.

By the end of the book you will have a:-

- Clear and specific law topic;

- Law thesis;

- Clear list of issues you want to explore in your dissertation;

- Clear idea of the practical application of your area of law;

- Plan for the research method[s] you will use.

You will also find a FREE checklist and PPT slides to help you with law dissertation at www.inspiredtostudy.org You can also book a FREE consultation, to discuss whether you would benefit from your own study coach to provide dissertation advice and feedback.

1.

READ YOUR ASSESSMENT CRITERIA AND RULES BEFORE YOU CHOOSE YOUR LAW DISSERTATION

"If you don't understand the details of your business you are going to fail."

— JEFF BEZOS,

TECHNOLOGY AND RETAIL

ENTREPRENEUR

Most students are bombarded with a lot of written information when they start a new course. It is tempting to give these documents a quick glance and then move on to the important task of choosing your dissertation subject. This is **Mistake no. 1** and the worst mistake you can make because you are **failing to consider how you can maximise your marks.**

The key to writing a top law dissertation is to make sure that your dissertation scores maximum points in every category of the marking criteria. If you have not read and identified the key scoring areas you cannot adapt your dissertation to maximise your marks. If you have read the marking criteria and then disregard them you are not maximising your potential. For most students getting a good grade is the number one reason for writing their law dissertation.

STUDENT EXPERIENCE- JOHN

John came to our first supervision session, keen to tell me about his dissertation subject and plans. He had spent time working on his employment law dissertation proposal, which involved a recent Supreme Court case report. He had read this recent judgment. The problem with this plan was there was no available research to show the effect of this new caselaw or for him to show his research skills in this area. His proposed dissertation was predominately based on his analysis of one case and his opinion on how employment law practices would change in the future.

The assessment criteria however required him to demonstrate an awareness and evaluation of current legal principles. He had to demonstrate an ability to carry out legal research and to show that he could evaluate several legal authorities.

I started with one question. "John how will your dissertation fit the research assessment criteria?" He looked at me as if I was deliberately trying to ask him a trick question. He sat back in his chair and began to think. Finally, he said "...erm ...I am not sure. That's NOT a question that I've considered." John added "...I see that this is something important that I should have checked." This was an important lesson for him to learn BEFORE his plans and research had been finalised. John now had time to refine dissertation title and content so that he could demonstrate all his skills and obtain that amazing final grade.

Those students who get the best grades are usually those who have identified what they are required to do under the assessment criteria and then delivered it. They are the students who have planned, organised their research and content for their law dissertation to maximise marks under every part of the assessment criteria. The general rule is that it is easier to score higher grades if you obtain a high average for every criterion, rather than doing well in one or two areas and poorly in others.

Your job at this stage is to consider yourself on a special mission, one that requires planning, strategy and consistent application until the task is complete. **I want you to actually read your assessment criteria and rules for your law dissertation course. Your focus is on the key words that describe the different classifications for a dissertation award and the standard required for each classification.**

Your University will have generic assessments and marking schemes which your department may adapt or modify for their own courses. You need to make sure you are reading the assessment criteria and marking scheme **for your specific course**. These are often found on your department/course website. You may also be given a written copy at the beginning of the course or when your dissertation course materials are distributed.

You should find the **grade description** and **marking criteria** for each grade classification. Here you are paying attention to the difference between dissertations that are awarded the top grade, usually a distinction and those obtaining the grade below, usually a merit or commendation grade.

The grade descriptors will normally cover the following areas:

- Research and methodology

- Quality of independent research

- Engagement with content, critical analysis and evaluation

- Quality and clarity of arguments

- Complexity of issues and originality of ideas

- Structure, presentation and written style of dissertation

- Bibliography and referencing

The grade descriptors should be written in such a way that you clearly understand the difference between each grade. If you don't then this is the time to email your supervisor and ask for clarification of any descriptors you think are unclear. If your law dissertation is marked out of 100 you will usually need to score 70 or above (or the equivalent of 70%) to fall within the range distinction classification. You need to identify the score for your own course.

Here is what I recommend you do once you have your grade descriptors.

TASK ONE

- READ your course assessment marking criteria and grade descriptors.

- COMPLETE the two tables below.

- IDENTIFY & RECORD the key words used for the top grade and then for a merit/commendation grade.

You will find that some of the words used overlap and apply to both grades, but you should find that there are some descriptions that only apply to a distinction grade.

- INSERT in the final column only those words that apply to the **quality or standard to be achieved for a distinction grade.** For example, descriptors for both grades will refer to research but the distinction descriptor will indicate a higher quality or standard to be reached. For example, if the descriptor describes the standard as "excellent research, capable of publication". Here the words to record are "excellent research".

Have a look at a completed example in Appendix B if you are unsure how to complete the tables below.

Table A

Top law dissertation descriptors	Grade Range	Qualitative /standard for distinction classification

Table B

Merit/Commendation descriptors	Grade Range	Qualitative/standard for Merit/Commendation classification

Task Two

Answer the following questions:

1. Can you see any **similarities between a distinction and merit/commendation grade**? What are they? List them in your work book or note App.

2. Record at least **5 major differences in the quality or standard** expected to be reached for a top law dissertation.

3. What have you learned by completing this exercise? Write it down.

Summary

- The key to writing a top law dissertation is to make sure that your dissertation scores maximum points in **every category** of the assessment marking criteria.

- If you have not read and **identified the key scoring areas,** you cannot design your law dissertation to the marking standard. You should be able to identify the key descriptors and marks that distinguish a distinction classification from a merit/commendation grade.

2.

FOLLOW YOUR PASSION AND YOU WILL FIND YOUR MOTIVATION.

"The question I ask everyday...how much further can I stretch to reach my fullest potential?"

— **OPRAH WINFREY, MEDIA PROPRIETOR, AUTHOR & PHILANTHROPIST**

N ow it is time to focus on YOU and why you have chosen to study your chosen area of law. What do you like about the subject? Why do YOU find it so fascinating? If you were stuck on a broken down train which law books would you want to have with you? These are personal questions that only you can answer. Students who are engaged have a genuine passion in exploring their law dissertation thesis. They produce well researched, intellectually challenging and thought-provoking law dissertations.

TASK 3

Record what you find fascinating about your dissertation subject and why you love it.

1.

2.

3.

4.

5.

DEFINING YOUR PASSIONS

Some students confuse an interest in a subject with real passion for a subject. An interest is something that gets your attention, but it does not last long. Sooner or later you will find a distraction and your interest may wane. You will find doing something else far more enjoyable. **If you have a real passion for a subject you will stick at the task–distractions will tempt you, but you will push them aside and keep going.**

Mistake no.2 is not understanding what you really have a passion for and choosing a topic that will not keep you interested. If your passion for your subject is not sustained over the 9-12 months that it will take to plan, research and write your dissertation the consequences will be serious. **Boredom is the no 1 killer of top law dissertations.** This happens when a student has lost interest in their subject. These students start to run out of motivation, they start to just want to get the task done and their standards drop. Worse they may never finish their dissertation, abandoning the task altogether. Disengaged students produce boring, uninteresting, routine practice-focused law dissertations.

Students who are engaged have a genuine passion in exploring their law dissertation thesis. They produce well researched, intellectually challenging and thought-provoking law dissertations. The enthusiasm of the student infiltrates the research, planning and writing of the dissertation. I have marked many dissertations: the difference between the two types of dissertation are obvious to the examiner.

Sometimes lack of interest in a topic makes some students question whether they have chosen the right topic. These students are more likely to want to change the focus of their dissertation or start a new topic. This is really an attempt to inject some motivation into their work. Each of these steps will have serious consequences because it means a student, having invested considerable time, energy and work, is now abandoning that work and striking out in a different direction. The inevitable consequence is that they have less time and the same amount of work to complete. These students often fall behind in their timetable. They may have to reduce the scope of their law dissertation to save time and endure much higher levels of stress in their bid to try and catch up.

In everyday life there are many choices you must make. There are hundreds of tasks that distract you from other tasks that you may want to do each day. The human mind has an amazing ability to help and hinder your best laid plans. Your motivation is your greatest weapon in driving you forward to plan, research and write your top law dissertation. **Your task must be to make sure that you chose a subject, topic and thesis that you really have a passion for. This is the time to sort out the things you have a passing interest in from the stuff that really sets you on fire and motivates you.**

STRETCHING YOUR KNOWLEDGE

An important part of motivation is 'stretching' your knowledge. This means working beyond your current knowledge and past achievements. If you are motivated, you will always want to 'stretch' your knowledge so you acquire a better understanding of your subject. Have you ever studied a topic that you can't get enough information about? You feel like a sponge: the more knowledge you acquire the more you want. Time seems to fly by and your research seems effortless.

You need to be intellectually challenged by your law dissertation topic, remember this is not the time to "read and repeat" (reading information that you have previously acquired and re-packaging it, so you are just repeating what you have done before). In your dissertation you will be looking for new and challenging arguments, ideas and theories. You will be analysing, interpreting and developing your own theories on your research data. Studying a subject that you are passionate about and having the desire to find out more will fuel your motivation to produce exceptional work.

STUDENT EXPERIENCE–ROHAN

Rohan, a former law student, had completed an undergraduate law dissertation. For his post-graduate LLM dissertation he thought it would be a good idea to develop his undergraduate dissertation subject. He thought this would be an easy way of doing his LLM dissertation. The problem was that significant parts of his dissertation simply mirrored a lot of his undergraduate work.

The work was no longer fresh or interesting to Rohan. He began to lack the desire to finish his work. In short, he had become bored. Rohan decided he just couldn't continue with his dissertation.

I don't want this to happen to you so choose your law dissertation topic carefully.

- What are you passionate about?

- What really fires your imagination?

- What 'stretches' you to find out more?

Choose a topic that is current, there is nothing worse than a student who chooses a subject and topic that has been done many times before. When you review previous law dissertations that have been produced you may find that a topic has been chosen by several students over the last few years. When you choose a topic that is stale then it is hard to find anything new and innovative to write.

Current and topical law may not always appear at first to be exciting. Try to find those topics that are current and relevant to your practice area where you can have an innovative approach. For example, e-disclosure and costs in civil-litigation may not seem interesting or topical but when you consider the requirements for costs saving measures and the development of artificial intelligence to carry out routine tasks this topic suddenly looks more interesting. How will AI impact on disclosure in the future? Will robots be expected and trusted to complete disclosure? **Remember a practice-focused dissertation being topical, current and original are likely to be part of the assessment criteria. "Read and repeat" law dissertations do not score high on originality or demonstrate complex research skills.**

Time to ask yourself–is this subject and topic still current? Do I have anything new to add to the discussion? If you are simply going to document and repeat what others have written–it is time to 'stretch' yourself in a different direction.

TASK 4

Stage One

Complete the table below from 1-7, by first entering your preliminary law subject[s] and then two or three topic ideas in that subject. Try to do this exercise quickly without thinking about it too much. Here you are trying to tap into what you instinctively feel about the subject and topic. Look at the example I have completed below.

Table C

Subject [1]	Topic or working title [2]	Interest level (very high) [3]	Interest level (high)	Can I study this for 9 months? (Yes/No) [4]	Current & Innovative? (Yes / No) [5]	Stretch factor (Yes /No) [6]	Shortlisted (Yes /No) [7]
1. Law- litigation - disclosure	Part 31 CPR–is it a force for good?		✓	Yes	No Lots done on this topic	No ? broad topic ? lots of research in this area	No
	Is disclosure too expensive for clients & modern law businesses?	✓		Yes	Yes	No wide subject to research- research from client and business perspective	No
	Is the future of litigation e-disclosure and the use of AI to save costs?	✓		Yes	Yes	Yes Current, topical and depth for detailed research. Innovation	Yes ✓
2. Law– clinical negligence	Disclosure– can practitioner get a fair		✓	Yes	No–broad subject been covered	No Not topical or current No	No

	hearing with current disclosure rules?				before	innovative angle	
3. Now it is your turn -start here							
4.							
5.							

TASK 5

Stage Two

Wait 24 hours and then it is time to test your choices using the **stack and throw principle.** Using only the topics/working titles in columns 2 above (forget the topics you have shortlisted in column 7 of the table above)

This is simple:

1. Stack the contender topics in column 2 in order. **Start with your least favourite at the bottom and work your way up to your favourite at the top.** Don't look at how you graded or shortlisted these topic, in the table above. **Then review your list and choose and throw out the bottom two subjects. Put a line through them.**

2. **Repeat the process.**

3. Gradually work your way up the list until you are left with your top two topics/working titles. **Disregard anything that is not in the top two on the list.**

Now it is time to sit back and think about your selections. The topics/working titles you shortlist in stage one should be the same shortlisted in the stack and throw process. If you have achieved this in both tasks, then you have identified two topics that you are passionate about and motivated to study.

If you chose different topics in task 4 and 5 this simply highlights that you are still unsure of what you want to study and where your true passion lies. Read on and come back to this exercise after you have read chapter four. Repeat the exercise.

Summary

- Your strategy is to choose a subject and topic that you feel genuinely passionate about and motivated to study.

- Your strategy is to find a subject that 'stretches' your intellectual abilities and sustain your interest for the next 9-12 months as you carry out your research, planning and writing.

- Your strategy is to find something new, innovative and current about your practice-focused law dissertation, so you can maximise marks in every category.

3.

Consider ALL reasons for writing your law dissertation.

"Everything is possible when you unlock your potential and step into your success."

— **Suzanne Reece**

Mistake no.3 is forgetting to think about all the reasons for writing your practice-focused law dissertation. Do this and you will fail to consider some very important factors. Your academic guidance notes will suggest that you choose your dissertation topic carefully. They will recommend you choose a subject that you are passionate about. **Your law dissertation is also a tool that has a lot of other important uses once you complete your course. Your task is to make your law dissertation work for you in as many ways as possible by having more than one purpose.** Today students are much more astute in using their time, hard work and intelligence to upcycle their practice-focused law dissertation to have more than one purpose.

Here are 10 uses for your law dissertation, apart from your current course:-

i.   It may form the **basis of higher academic study**, for example further masters study. I am not suggesting you write the same dissertation twice but some of the research may be used as a foundation to explore the subjects in a different direction that you could not address in your first dissertation.

ii.   It may be **relevant to a future practice-focused law course** that you wish to study. Your law dissertation may be used as part of your supporting statement for an advanced professional course application or specialist accreditation.

iii.   It may be **relevant to future employment**. Imagine if your law dissertation topic has some relevance to the type of law you intend to practise. You may use it to distinguish yourself from other job applicants and/or as a point of discussion at future job interviews. For example, if you choose a topic that is current and relevant to your future employment this is an amazing tool to show that you already have a lot of detailed knowledge on the subject and to suggest you may be ahead of other candidates when it comes to future training.

iv.   You may wish to use your law dissertation as **research for a future business** venture. How many billionaires started their dot.com companies after an idea at university developed into viable business? Can you think of anyone? For example, combine your law dissertation with another discipline such as business or intellectual property law. Use your law dissertation to form the basis of supporting evidence **for obtaining finance**, for example by **crowd-funding for a new project, business or joint venture**. What better research than to implement a business theory, test and measure the results and produce a tangible business proposition that you can then use to model a new start-up?

v.   If your dissertation also covers a topic that relates to a hobby or special interest, you may use it to **enhance your reputation as an expert** in that field. For example, you may be studying law and have an interest in photography, wildlife and travel. Could a law dissertation combining your academic subject and hobbies be used to help you build a portfolio for your photography and international travel by creating a specialist blog?

vi.   Your law dissertation may be **turned into a resource such as a book** which you self-publish or submit for **academic**

publication. You may make your book freely available to the public by open publishing. In a time when students publish blogs, build communities using their Facebook pages and other social media channels, how great would it be to turn your first dissertation into a book or resource that worked for you?

vii. Form the **basis for future collaboration** in the academic or non-academic context. Many people use their social media or printed work as their business cards. Your dissertation may tell people something about you. People with similar interests reach out and make connections and form collaborations with people because of what they see, hear or read.

viii. Form the basis for **setting up a not-for-profit organisation, charity or social enterprise.** Today people do not wait for others to set up social enterprises where they feel there is a lack of resources. Your research could help you and others to understand, prepare and devise new social enterprises to meet community needs. For example, an advice centre or pro bono organisation.

ix. Use it to **set up a new NGO, network, campaign or lobby group** with people that share an interest in your area of law to help campaign for a change in legislation, highlight judicial decisions or seek to establish new rights—for example, a community legal action group-the list of groups is endless.

x. Finally, you could do none of the above, simply produce your law dissertation and then put it in a drawer and never look at it again.

Universities and prospective employers look for similar qualities in students: academic ability, engagement and ability to stand out. Students stand out from the crowd by organising, creating and engaging in things that they are passionate about. They can also demonstrate this ability in their written work. Your practice-focused dissertation can be your way of showing that you stand out from the crowd.

For example, I was at a law careers event when I was approached by a group of female law students. I had spoken on the panel about the need for students to stand out from the crowd to prospective law firms. They approached me at the end of the event and asked, "How can we stand out from the crowd?" I asked them what type of law they were interested in practising and what attempts they had made to get work experience in this field.

They told me they were passionate about European law. There was no student network group for this area of law, so they had set up their own group at Coventry University. They established contact with other universities which had similar European law student societies and established links with professional European lawyers' groups in the UK. My advice: "Keep doing what you are doing." This group were standing out from the crowd by showing that they were committed to a specialist area of law, could problem solve, network and establish strategic partnerships with European lawyers in the UK; just the sort of skills a progressive law firm would love to see in their trainee solicitors. Your practice-focused dissertation can show that you stand out from the crowd.

TASK SIX

Answer the following questions and record your answers:

1. Are you going to put your law dissertation in a drawer and forget about it? Yes or No.

2. Can you identify and record at least 3 non-course related uses for YOUR completed law dissertation? This will depend on your personal goals. The list above may help but you may have different goals.

3. If you can't answer question 2 it is time to pause, think about your short and medium-term plans. Do some research on what grades, qualifications or experience you need to achieve future plans.

4. How are you going to use your law dissertation to stand out from the crowd in your post graduate life?

5. If you have not completed Task 5 go back and complete it now.

You will also find a FREE checklist and PPT slides to help you with your practice-focused law dissertation to download at www.inspiredtostudy.org You can also book a FREE consultation, to discuss whether you would benefit from your own study coach.

SUMMARY

- Your task is to make your law dissertation work for you in as many ways as possible by having more than one purpose.

- You need to choose a subject that meets:-

  - the assessment marking criteria

  - your course specification criteria

  - your interest and passion for the subject

  - your personal non-course related future goals

4.

IDENTIFY THE ISSUES YOUR DISSERTATION WILL COVER AT AN EARLY STAGE.

"In my opinion, there is no aspect of reality beyond the reach of the human mind."

STEPHEN HAWKINS,
FORMER PHYSICIST, COSMOLOGIST
AND AUTHOR

You have selected your broad subject and may have an idea of the working title. Now it is time to delve into that detailed literature review, or is it?

Many students at this stage plunge into their research and after some time they begin to get confused, go off on topics that are not central to their law dissertation thesis. At this early stage you need to focus your reading so as to go into the right amount of detail in the right areas. If you have not decided on a structure for your reading by identifying the issues, how will you ever navigate through the volumes of potential reading?

How do you stay on track and on top of the issues? **Before, during and at the end of your research you must have a clear idea of the core issues that you are going to deal with in your dissertation.** You need a dissertation or research plan. **Mistake no. 4 is not having a detailed idea of the issues that your law dissertation will cover at an early stage.**

Think of this as the content page of your law dissertation, it is the roadmap and plan that will help you navigate the areas that you will discuss in your dissertation. If you have not thought about what issues you will need to address and produced a plan for yourself there is a real risk that you will start reading and keep reading. You run the risk of getting lost in the massive amount of information that you will discover when carrying out your literature review.

Most students sketch out a broad and general plan of the issues that the dissertation will cover but what you need is much more detail to keep you on track. The difference is between setting out on a journey knowing that you are vaguely heading in a northerly direction, as opposed to having a map showing you how to get to a destination.

The strategy is to fit your research to the list of issues that your dissertation requires. Your proposal will have set out the general areas you propose to cover. Now it is time to produce a more detailed dissertation or research plan. This is very much like preparing your essay plan. Your plan will focus on the obvious topics and issues for each chapter. Your research may lead you to additional issues, so you will need to keep your plan under review. Unlike your essay plan this dissertation or research plan will need to be more flexible because as you carry out your research you will need to update it.

At this stage you are going to need to read and understand the main legal principles, caselaw and arguments on which your main subject is based. You may find additional issues that are repeatedly discussed in legal commentaries or interviews. You may find new data or new cases that have a significant impact on the issues. As you research, you may find you want to add or eliminate some of the periphery or broader issues (not your core issues!) from your list. **Your list of issues is not a static list, it can and should develop with your research.**

Robert, one of my workshop students had a problem. He had carried out his literature review and was deep into his research but really felt he didn't know when to stop. He asked: "When do I know that I have enough research for my dissertation?" My reply to Robert:

1. Do you have a list of issues you planned to cover?

2. Did you revise and add to this list as you carried out your research?

3. Can you go back over your current list of issues and tick off research that comprehensively deals with every issue?

If you can answer yes to the three questions above, then you have done enough research.

Finally, at the end of your research you should pause, reflect and evaluate your research. Compare it with the latest list of issues that you have and as you reflect, consider whether you have missed an important issue or failed to develop an issue to its conclusion. This is the time when, if you feel your law dissertation is lacking in a specific area, you can top up the subject with more research. If you are happy with your research and it covers all the issues you wanted to address, congratulations, it is time to move on to the next stage.

IDENTIFYING YOUR DISSERTATION TITLE

At this stage you may have a dissertation title, but many students wait until they have finalised their research before settling on their final title for submission. At this stage a working title is fine. Many universities will have a deadline for the submission of the final dissertation title so make sure you submit this in time.

If your university requires you to submit your dissertation title before you complete your research then this is stage that you have invest time in the preparatory stages; sorting out the subject, issues, title and carry out a preliminary literature review [chapters 2-7]. Your aim at this stage will be to produce a dissertation title that reflects the issues you have chosen to address in your dissertation. **The title will need to set a question or proposition that you will address in the dissertation AND answer!**

If you don't have to submit your final dissertation title until you have completed your research then you have the added benefit of being able to refine your title after you have completed your research.

The process of conducting your research, refining the issues you are going to address and working out your final dissertation title is a process that takes time. Very few students start with all the answers at the beginning of their research. **What you are striving for is the evolution of your ideas, refining the issues and then finding the title that perfectly reflects the content of your research. The title will need to set a question or proposition that you will address in the dissertation AND answer!**

SUMMARY

1. The purpose of your research is to help you understand and clarify the areas you will cover in your law dissertation. If you spend time thinking and planning before you start your research, you will have a clearer idea of what issues you need to cover.

2. Your plan will need to be revised and updated as you research.

3. At the end of your research pause, reflect and evaluate your

research. Your research should reflect the question or proposition you posed in your dissertation title AND provide an ANSWER.

5.

IDENTIFY A THESIS QUESTION WORTHY OF AN EXCEPTIONAL DISSERTATION.

"Excellence is never an accident; it is the result of ...intelligent direction and skilful execution."

— ANONYMOUS

Having identified the topics and issues that you are going to cover it is necessary to identify the thesis question you are going to address in your dissertation. The thesis you are going to test will be the focus of your research and written work. You will discuss, challenge and set out your own opinions on this important question.

There is one golden rule when setting your thesis question, "**Go big or go home**". Simply put, if you are just going to describe the latest cases, legal principles or legislation on your chosen subject you might as well go home. There is nothing challenging, interesting or engaging about a practice-focused law dissertation that does no more than repeat and explain. **Mistake no. 5 is failing to set a challenging thesis question.** Describing a series of legal cases is not formulating a thesis question.

These are students who play it safe by choosing to keep things simple. They choose a very straightforward thesis and spend their time describing what other people have written on the subject. These dissertations are more like extended essays than dissertations. They do show a degree of legal knowledge and that the student has spent time understanding legal concepts. They don't demonstrate excellent research, innovation or a novel way of looking at a practice-focused legal subject.

Some students move to the next stage, by introducing an element of analysis, but they play it safe. They limit their thesis either to comparing similarities or finding differences. This is the "compare or contrast two relatively simple concepts" type of dissertation. Again, this has the same problem as my first example, it is a thesis that fails to demonstrate the intellectual "stretch" required of an exceptional practice-focused law dissertation. The best way to demonstrate this is to show you some examples of how choosing the right thesis question begins the process of getting higher marks.

EXAMPLES OF TYPES OF DISSERTATIONS

Example A

A law student writes a dissertation comparing the legal systems of England and Bangladesh. The working title is:

"An analysis of the legal systems of England and Bangladesh"

Here the student may cover the historical development of each legal system, how the law is developed in each jurisdiction and look at the similarities of the two systems. This is essentially a descriptive law dissertation. There is some analysis of the two systems, in discussing their similarities, but it does not require a great deal of innovative thought, research or complexity.

Example B

Assume the same topic as above, but the student introduces more complexity to the dissertation. This time she will compare and contrast the two legal systems and introduce a thesis which will require consideration of a third jurisdiction. The working title is:

"The English and Bangladeshi legal systems fail to address the need for swiftly developing case law in the modern era of rapid technological development, a problem solved by European Union law (EU) and Regulations."

Now we can see that this topic is going to require the student to do more than just describe the historical development and current legal systems in England, Bangladesh and the EU. There is the introduction of the idea of that two of these legal systems don't cope well with swiftly developing case law especially with new technological developments. Inevitably this dissertation will need to compare, contrast and evaluate how this requirement is dealt with in each jurisdiction by highlighting some of the leading cases. The student will need to support the proposition that the system in the EU is better and more successful at adapting to the need for changing law. This will require the student to devise a framework against which all three jurisdictions can be compared, measured and judged.

The student will also need to show how modern technologies are developing at such a pace that new legislation has to be implemented quickly. A discussion of how current legislation and caselaw is implemented to cope with the challenges will need to be discussed. This type of dissertation is now a modern, innovative and a current analysis of legal practice. There is also the opportunity to use examples from modern tech companies to illustrate the thesis question: by showing how recent legal developments have impacted on the way these companies conduct business.

This topic gives the student the opportunity to combine traditional and modern research techniques. Research on legal principles, legislation and caselaw can follow traditional research methods but there is also the opportunity to use modern research methods; for example social media, vlogs and blogs.

Example C

Example C demonstrates how the right dissertation title can really help a student focus on a specific area of legal research.

Again, we will use the same subject. The new working title is:

"The development of modern tech companies has left many workers without vital employment rights and benefits—An analysis of the effect of Uber on employment rights in England, Bangladesh and the EU."

In this example, we are not considering the whole legal system just a specific area of law dealing with employment right and benefits for individuals. Focusing the dissertation on employment rights allows the student to go into greater detail on this topic. There is the need to compare, evaluate and discuss the effect of Uber's practices in the three jurisdictions by considering the leading employment rights cases. Finally, the student must define and discuss how current law affects workers and leaves them "...without vital employment rights and benefits."

Example D

Example D shows how a thesis can present a positive and negative proposition for discussion. The working title is:

"Are modern tech companies a force for change and development? Or are they a force that needs to be controlled by legislation for the benefit of their workers? An analysis of the effect of Uber on employment rights of workers in England, Bangladesh and France."

The above working title now introduces an additional dimension that requires the student to discuss the concept of "change and development" and whether the changes in employment practices are a force for good. The comparable legal jurisdictions have now been refined to selecting just one country in the European Union, France.

The key is to remember if you choose a broad theme with lots of issues then the reality is that you will not be able to cover your topics and issues in detail. The danger is that you produce a practice-focused law dissertation that only discusses the issues generally. Overall a dissertation that lacks detailed analysis is less likely to get the top marks.

In contrast, if you choose a narrower topic with fewer issues (but don't go too far and reduce the issues to one or two so you make it too simplistic!) then you will be able to take your investigations and research much deeper. The more detailed your research, the more complex arguments you can pursue.

Try to think of this dilemma like a swimming pool. You are on holiday and there are two pools in the hotel. One is a nice large pool, but it is quite shallow, you can paddle around but it is no good for diving. The other pool is smaller, but it is very deep and excellent for diving. These pools are like your dissertations–the shallow pool represents those dissertations that deal with the subject and issues in a very general and broad way. The deep pool represents those students who are able to narrow their topic and issues, so they can allocate their research and time to looking at very detailed and complex arguments. You must choose what type of law dissertation you want to produce but those dissertations that dive deep into complex issues are more likely to score those top grades.

Task Seven

Time to start refining the thesis question or proposition for your practice-focused law dissertation.

Start with your preferred topic and broad working title:

1. List the issues you think you need to cover (this is your content page).

2. Devise a working title for your dissertation [title 1].

3. Think of ANOTHER working title, similar but different from your first choice. The title will reflect the topic and issues you have chosen but with a slightly different focus [title 2].

4. Refine both working titles by producing another two titles [titles 3 & 4]. Try to narrow the subject. Find the current and innovative issues worthy of that distinction grade.

5. You should now have 4 working titles. Put them on your desk or laptop where you will see them regularly.

6. A week later reflect on these titles. Has your research and passion steered you towards one of the titles? Eliminate the two titles that you least like and choose a title from the remaining two.

You can also book a FREE consultation, to discuss whether you would benefit from your own study coach:

www.inspiredtostudy.org

SUMMARY

- Choosing the right thesis question or proposition is as important as choosing your subject.

- Try to narrow your topic and issues so you can focus your research on the more challenging propositions. The more detailed your research, the more complex arguments you can pursue.

- Try to compose at least 4 different working titles and then gradually select the one title that best fits your research, content and aims.

6.

TEST IT BEFORE YOU USE IT

"If you can't explain it simply, you don't understand it well enough."

— ALBERT EINSTEIN

aving identified at least two topics that you find interesting and identified your non-course related reasons for writing your practice-focused law dissertation, it is time to do some preliminary research to see if the topics are viable for your dissertation. **Your preliminary literature review is key to helping you decide which is the right topic for you at the planning stage before you invest time in a full literature review. Mistake no.6 is not testing your topic before you use it.** Getting the preliminary literature review wrong may lead you to choose a topic that does not allow you to maximise scores across all categories of the assessment criteria.

WHAT IS A PRELIMINARY REVIEW?

This is NOT a full literature review but a short "tester" for your research. You are checking the quality of the research available for two potential working titles and then assessing which will help you maximise marks. The preliminary review has to satisfy the "5-Purpose test" set out below.

THE "5-PURPOSE TEST"

Purpose no.	The 5-Purpose test for your preliminary literature review
1	To discover if there is **sufficient research material to**

	make the topic academically rigorous for an exceptional law dissertation. Consider the quality and access to existing research for your independent study.
2	To establish whether this topic will allow you to obtain **maximum marks in every category of the assessment marking criteria.** Go back to the notes you made on the key descriptors and assessment grades for a top law dissertation grade.
3	To establish whether the subject is **current and topical** for a practice-focused dissertation. If it is NOT how can you find a way to make it current?
4	To identify how you can bring an **innovative approach** to your law dissertation.
5	To identify what **type of research** you will need to carry out. How are you practically going to carry out that research? How long will it take? Identify any potential problems and delays.

The purpose of this test is to establish:

- Whether your first preference is the right topic for you.

- If your first preference doesn't pass the 5-Purpose test you will realise this at the planning stage, rather than weeks later after you have invested time and effort in a formal literature review.

- If your first choice doesn't work out AND your second

choice does you will realise this should be your first choice.

- If both choices pass the 5-Purpose test you are in a win-win scenario and really can choose either topic.

How to carry out a Preliminary Literature Review

Start with your preferred topic or working title and then repeat it for your second-choice topic or working title. DON'T spend lots of time reading about the details of your topics; you will do this in the full literature review. You do not need lots of notes and records at this stage.

You are looking for the following information:

- **Broadly review the main (no more than 5-10) books on your legal subject on the two topics you have selected.** You are looking at the content pages, chapters and appendices to get an overall idea of the data and research available for you to use in the future. You are collating a list of primary and secondary sources that are available for further investigation.

- You are identifying the **quantitative data** that is available or maybe identifying that there is NO quantitative data. Is there any public or government statistical evidence to help you? Consider research published by professional bodies such as the Bar Standards Board and The Law Society, both these organisations produce Annual Statistics Reports. Can you conduct polls, surveys or have access to anonymised feedback results? Check the date of your research material - is it current? This does not mean that it must have been produced yesterday, data takes time to be published but generally if you are going to write a current practice-focused dissertation you are hoping to find research material that is no more than to 2 or 3 years old.

- You will be thinking about the **qualitative data** that you can realistically obtain. Here think about in-depth interviews and case observations. Alternatively you may think of helping with pro bono cases and then writing reflective notes. Do you have contacts, friends or family that can help with access to individuals to interview? Think about how you will obtain your research, process the information, compare and evaluate results.

- If your research is going to focus on an **analysis of legislation and caselaw** consider the relevant primary and secondary sources. How are they relevant to your dissertation topic?

- Check the source of the data. Is it reputable, credible and appropriate for academic study? What research tools are available? Consider traditional library-based research and online research tools?

- Does the topic provide sufficient academic rigour? Remember you are beyond the stage of "describe and explain". You are looking for a project that will involve complex analysis of the issues. A subject that will "test and conclude" "analyse and devise solutions". A title and topic that will pose and ANSWER the dissertation question.

If you are still confused about which working title to choose **obtain a second opinion**. Speak to your supervising tutor and see what she/he has to say. What you want to know is which of the two potential topics would give you the better opportunity to demonstrate your skills under the assessment criteria. Look at the words in bold below because these are the areas that you need to consider.

- Quality of independent **research.**

- Engagement with **content, critical analysis and evaluation.**

- **Quality** and clarity of arguments.

- **Complexity of issues,** and

- **Originality of ideas.**

Your University library will have excellent research sheets to demonstrate how you should conduct legal research. Make sure that you read them as this will save time when you start your research. Libraries will often have designated law librarians that can help you with any research problems and direct you to useful resources. They often run training courses on how to use legal resources so book an early appointment.

Inns of court and The Law Society have their own libraries and useful online resources that you can access. For example, check out https://www.accesstolaw.com where you will find legal resources selected & annotated by Inner Temple Library. This is a gateway site, providing links to selected UK, Commonwealth and worldwide free legal websites. Middle Temple Library also provides access to a number of useful law website and their "Links for lawyers page" has access to practice focused law portals & legal Apps. Check out https://www.middletemple.org.uk/library-and-archive/library/electronic-resources. The Law Society has an extensive library and a useful online library search that you can access at https://wv-tls.olib.oclc.org/webview/.

How long should your Preliminary review take?

"How long is a piece of string?" The answer is it depends … it should not be as long as a formal literature review. You preliminary review should be long enough for you to find the answers to the 5-Purpose test. When you have the answers STOP!

Summary

- Choose your top two working titles for your law dissertation and then test them.

- When you have found the right topic and two potential working titles , test them before you commit to one.

- A preliminary review will help you decide if your preferred topic meets the 5-Purpose test.

7.

FORM YOUR OWN OPINIONS AND DISCUSS THEM IN YOUR DISSERTATION.

"...your success will be determined by your own confidence and fortitude."

— **MICHELLE OBAMA, FORMER USA FIRST LADY, LAWYER AND PHILANTHROPIST**

Every author has to carefully research the issues and you will find that there are at least two competing views on most issues. Have you heard the expression: "there are always two sides to an argument"? When you ask six lawyers the same question you are likely to find six slightly different answers! When you carry out your research you will carefully record and reference these opposing views.

Clear logical work is produced when you carefully evaluate both sides to an argument. You need to analyse the strength and weakness of each argument. Second test and challenge what you have read. When you have done this, you can analyse the success or accuracy of the arguments you have researched and begin to develop the arguments that form your thesis.[1]

There is one further step you need to take. To get the higher grades, you need to move beyond testing and challenging the arguments. You need to draw your own conclusions, comment on what you have read and find your own views based on your research. **Mistake no. 7 is not finding your own opinions.** Many students struggle with this part of their law dissertation; they do not feel that they have the right to comment and draw conclusions on the issues. This is wrong: if you have done the research and put in the hard work you have the right to comment on the legal issues.

---

[1] You may like to read 10 Reasons You Didn't Write an Outstanding Opinion to help with your critical thinking and analysis skills in legal writing.

TASK EIGHT

A good way to get yourself into the right zone for this kind of thinking is, after researching a topic or issue, at the end your note ADD THREE final questions and fill in the answers:

1. Having read… [you fill in the blank] **What do YOU think about what you have just read?** Do you agree or disagree?

2. Do you have **any additional ideas on this topic?**

3. **What is your conclusion on this issue?**

Explain why you have reached your conclusion and **show how your research supports this.**

Consider your three questions AND answers as soon as you finish your reading. If you leave a blank space and come back to the questions another day you may find them harder to answer. This is because you begin to doubt your answers are right. When you get completely absorbed in your research: you are thinking, analysing, processing the arguments. This is the best time for you to record your own ideas and views. This is the time when you spontaneously find yourself thinking and writing great things. If you are struggling to answer the questions, take a short break, go for a walk and see the answers fall into place when you return to your desk.

When you start to plan and write your law dissertation you will review your notes and may, during the editing stage, revise and update the opinions that you formed in the early stages. The important point is to make sure that your dissertation is not simply about the thoughts and opinions of published authors. **Your com-**

ments and opinions are important. Try wherever possible to support them by reference to your research as this adds credibility to your position.

Remember when we looked at the assessment criteria important marks are gained for your analysis and ideas. I have highlighted them below.

- Research and methodology.

- Quality of independent research.

- **Engagement with content, critical analysis and evaluation.**

- **Quality and clarity of arguments.**

- **Complexity of issues.**

- **Originality of ideas.**

- Structure, presentation and written style of dissertation.

- Bibliography and referencing.

TESTING YOUR IDEAS

Have you ever played chess or other board games by yourself? The object is to play your first move (or argument) and then turn the board and play as your opponent, blocking (or finding your counter-argument) for the first great move. See if you can find the flaws with the argument. When you are satisfied that you have demolished, undermined or weakened that argument with a counter-argument, turn the board again and find the weakness in the counter-argument.

A great way of testing how well you thought through your arguments, comments and conclusions is to debate the subject or issue with a friend or family member. Set out your arguments and get them to challenge you. See if they can find the weakness, illogical point or any irrelevance in the arguments you have set out in support of your position. Remember you need to support your arguments with your research. The challenge for you is not to just work in isolation but use your friends and family as a sounding board to test your thesis.

A word of warning—don't test your ideas and thesis with other students on your course doing a similar dissertation. Your dissertation must be your own work and you run the risk that if you produce similar ideas and arguments as another student there may be the suggestion that you worked together to produce your dissertation.

Don't miss supervision sessions with your tutor. These are great opportunities to discuss your opinions and conclusions. I always enjoyed these sessions with my students. This is when you really find out how well a student understands their subject and how well they have researched the issues and arguments. If my students could robustly and confidently defend the arguments in their draft chapters, in our supervision meeting, it was always a great sign. I knew this preparation would inevitably appear as persuasive written arguments in their final dissertation. Take the passion of the discussion and set it out in your well written arguments.

One word of warning for you. Make sure that the views you claim are yours and don't belong to someone else. It is important to make sure that the work of published authors is clearly referenced when you quote from them directly, paraphrase or summarise their views. You cannot claim the views of published authors are your own; this will lead to plagiarism allegations. Copying, stealing or using the work of published authors does not get you marks and is likely to lead to a disciplinary hearing and penalties when you are caught. The general principle is that if you are unsure, reference it. Make careful records of research and clearly identify the areas where you are expressing your own thoughts and opinions.

SUMMARY

- Elevate your grade by incorporating your comments and opinions on important topics and issues.

- Original ideas and thoughts get more marks so think about what you can add to the discussion and support it with your research.

- Test your thesis, debate with yourself, friends and family

8.

PLANNING, TIMING AND DELIVERY

"We have all the time in the world"

— **LOUIS ARMSTRONG, TRUMPETER**

AND SINGER

We have covered the seven key mistakes to avoid when selecting a practice-focused law dissertation, but I can't resist adding in number 8. This was one of the key stress points for many students and a mistake that can easily be avoided. Consider this the bonus point. **Mistake no. 8 is failing to properly understand how long it will take to plan, research and write your dissertation.**

You may think you have all the time in the world to complete your dissertation; most students have a whole year between submitting their proposal and handing in the finished dissertation. Mistake no. 8 is underestimating the time that it will take to plan, research and write your dissertation.

Universities will give you a timetable for submitting your dissertation proposal, drafts for supervision and your final law dissertation. Smart students will timetable the key dates into their study diaries and begin preparation early, so they submit their dissertation before the deadline day.

Mistake no. 8 is failing to schedule sufficient time for planning, researching, writing and completing your proposal and dissertation well in advance of the deadline. This must include time for the expected and unexpected problems and delays that may occur in researching and writing your dissertation. If you fail to properly plan and run into delays with research or writing, you may end up losing valuable marks.

In life it is important to plan for the unexpected. Sometimes you have no idea how long it will take to complete a task, so as a rule double whatever time you allocate to a task. Add extra time for tasks that are outside your control. Remember that despite your best efforts you may have to take time off because of illness, family matters or unexpected emergencies.

Here are some of the main stages when issues can throw students off track with their timetable:

Planning

Generally, this is within your control but what happens when you plan your proposal, carry out your preliminary literature review and then, as you start your literature review, you discover that some new legislation, procedure, protocol or data is being released that could change the way you research your topic? Your literature review should highlight this issue as commentaries and articles will often deal with new or impending changes that are about to come into effect.

A problem arises when new research data is published or new legislation comes into force after you have completed your planning and evaluation. You may have started writing your dissertation chapters. Leave some extra time to go back and address any new research, case law or legislation. You may be able to deal with new matters by inserting footnotes but sometimes you may have to add an extra paragraph or section on the new matter. If you are working to a dissertation deadline with no time to go back and update, your final evaluations and conclusions may well be flawed!

Research

This often takes longer than students expect. If you are collecting quantitative data, you need to look at the processes you are intending to use to collect this information. Even the most automated processes can require repeated reminders to be sent to participants, there can be delays in the collation process as you wait for final data and computer problems. Computer glitches, viruses and a failure to "back up" your work can cause delays in accessing your work.

In the case of qualitative data, interviews can be difficult to obtain with busy professionals and may have to be planned either at short notice or months in advance. If you are, for example interviewing members of the public, you need to consider how you will invite them to participate and where and when these interviews will take place, usually in a public venue for safety reasons. Again you may need more than one round of interviews if you don't get a sufficient number of participants.

Whether you are using quantitative or qualitative research you need to think about research ethics and whether you will need ethical approval for your proposed research. If you do there will normally be a panel or committee that considers these matters and this may take time. You will have to consider issues of confidentiality, the benefits to the clients in participating in the research and data protection of information. All of this needs to be considered before you start any research and discussed with your supervisor.

If your first round of research does not produce the quantity or quality of research that you anticipated, it is always good to have a plan B–your reserve and back-up. You will have to re-send your research questionnaires, polls, sample group testing or request new interviews. This takes time so always apply the general rules:

1. Assume that your research will take twice as long as you first estimate.

2. Always have a plan A & B.

3. Allow yourself time to implement plan B, if plan A doesn't
    work out.

REFERENCING

Your university will make it clear how they wish you to cite legislation, cases and reference sources–follow these rules and use them consistently throughout your dissertation and you will pick up easy marks.

Most legal authorities are cited using a standard method called the Oxford University Standard for the Citation of Legal Authorities. For more information and a free PDF check out https://www.law.ox.ac.uk/research-subject-groups/publications/oscola

Save time by making sure that you take careful notes of your reference sources you will not believe how time consuming it is to go back and find this information weeks or months later. Save even more time and compile your bibliography, list of statutes and cases as you research. This task is made so much easier if you use the reference tools provided Microsoft and Apple for citations and bibliographies allowing you to compile and edit these as you research and take notes.

Have a look at my top ten list of useful resources for legal research at Appendix D and remember to check out the resources offered by your own university.

EVALUATION

Your methodology will set out how you intend to research and evaluate your research data. Having collected your data, it is time to consider it and evaluate the results. If you have selected a quantitative approach for your research, you should have designed your data testing so that results are standardised, quantifiable and easy to compare. Students who do not take time to plan this process may struggle to collate, understand or evaluate the results that have been produced from the data they have collected.

The nightmare for any student is finding themselves confronted with a lot of data that they do not understand and struggle to evaluate. **Time spent planning how you are going to process, evaluate and use the data once you have collected it is just as important as obtaining your data. It is the classic problem that to be able successfully to use your research data you must start by planning how you will deal with the results.** The process of understanding and evaluating your data is critical to your research skills. Start with the end result, how you intend use the answers to your research and then plan backwards.

Qualitative research students, if they have not carefully devised a system for ordering their results, will find it time consuming to evaluate, compare and contrast the range of answers they obtain. For example, you decide to use interviews as your main source of collecting data based on a series of questions allowing participants to answer each question in their own words. How do you then compare and evaluate different answers that may have many different permutations? The key lies in thinking about the answers you are seeking and defining your questions so that the range of answers can be compared and evaluated. You may want lengthy answers for some questions but for others a short concise answer may be sufficient. For example, consider the two questions below and think about the potential range of answers to the different versions of the questions?

Sample Question 1

- How would you describe **your experience** of litigation? [option for lengthy answer]

- What **word** would **best describe your experience** of litigation? [one word option]

Sample Question 2

- How would you describe the **outcome of your litigation?** [option for lengthy answer]

- What **word would best describe the outcome of your litigation?** [one word option]

In the example above you need carefully to think whether you are trying to ascertain the **participant's experience** of litigation or their **views** on the outcome of their litigation. You need to consider whether you want to give the participant the option of a lengthy descriptive reply or a concise short answer.

WRITING YOUR DISSERTATION

Some students prefer to write each chapter of their dissertation as they complete their research, others prefer to wait until they have completed all their research and then write the whole dissertation. Whatever strategy you choose for writing your dissertation, your first draft is unlikely to be the final version you submit.

Most students will write a first draft, edit this and then may submit part of their work for their supervisor to comment on or to discuss in a supervision meeting. There is then a further re-reading of the relevant chapters, taking into consideration any supervision comments. There may be further editing and revisions before the chapter or dissertation is near its final version. Once you have the final chapter or dissertation there is the first, second and final spelling and grammar checks.

I would recommend you plan as a minimum:

- First draft

- Review and second draft

- Further review and final draft

At the end of this process you will have a detailed knowledge of your law dissertation, have considered every word you have written and edited your dissertation at least twice. This process of reviewing and editing is the way you achieve the precision, concision and clarity of argument that is essential in writing a distinctive law dissertation.

This process takes time and like any craft, taking a short cut lowers the quality of the work produced. If your dissertation deadline is approaching and you are more focused on completing the task, rather than making sure your analysis, writing and checking are the best they can bee your dissertation is likely to be compromised. Did you spot the spelling mistake in the last sentence? If you have carried out excellent research, it would be a shame if you you [another spelling error!] are unable to present the results, evaluation and written arguments in a logical and authoritative way because you have not had time to refine your written arguments, checked your spelling and presentation.

SHAUNA'S EXPERIENCE

Shauna, a university student who came to me for private advice and counselling had started her dissertation and then four months later had amended her proposal and decided to change her thesis. Her planning, research and dissertation writing began to fall behind her planned targets. Her assessments and final term assignments began to interrupt her law dissertation work. She began to experience extreme anxiety and stress, as she realised the extent of the tasks ahead. When I met her she was over-worked, not sleeping and very tearful.

My job was to help her deal with her anxiety and stress. I had to advise and help her work out an achievable and realistic revised timetable, that would meet her dissertation deadline and deal with her course work. Together we worked out the course work assignments that could be delayed and set up a new timetable to put her dissertation back on track.

There are limitations on when dissertation extensions can be granted, so don't assume that you can get a time extension for submitting your work. If you do submit your dissertation late, there may be strict rules about how late you can submit and often penalties for late submission; that increase with the delay. Late submission of a dissertation can lead to automatic reduction of marks, [between 5-10 marks] so make sure you understand the penalties that apply for a late submission in your law school. The quicker you realise there is a problem and get help, the longer you have to work on a solution.

You will find a FREE checklist and PPT slides to help you with your law dissertation to download at www.inspiredtostudy.org You can also book a FREE consultation, to discuss whether you would benefit from your own study coach.

SUMMARY

- It is essential to allocate enough time to write a top law dissertation

- Start early and have realistic plans for preparing, researching and writing your dissertation.

- A good plan includes a plan for delays, problems and the unexpected.

- When you have a plan—you are in control.

9.

SURVIVAL TIPS

"Survival can be summed up in three words – NEVER GIVE UP."

— BEAR GRYLLS, BRITISH ADVENTURER & SURVIVAL EXPERT

You are now well equipped to start your planning and research for your law dissertation. There are, however, a few tips I want you to watch out for over the coming months.

SURVIVAL TIP 1

At the beginning of this process, I want you to sit down and imagine what you are going to do when you submit your final dissertation. Imaging walking to the school office to hand in your dissertation or hitting the send key for your electronic submission! You have done a great job and feel amazing. Really imagine how you will feel…what an accomplishment. Think about the treat you will give yourself when you achieve this goal, just think about it.

When you feel overwhelmed by the tasks you have, think about this special day. As you work towards the deadline for submission think about this goal.

SURVIVAL TIP 2

All great journeys need preparation, **think of producing your law dissertation as a marathon rather than a quick sprint.** You want to start and maintain a good steady pace. A quick sprint and bolting off may see you running out of steam towards the end of the race.

The best preparation is drawing up a plan so that you do some work on your law dissertation over the whole length of your preparation time. Short bursts of work with long periods of doing nothing is rarely the most productive. Long periods of inactivity make it harder to restart and you spend a lot of time re-reading and re-thinking the information and knowledge that your memory has forgotten.

Pace yourself and do a little often rather than trying to do a lot and then having long gaps where you do nothing.

SURVIVAL TIP 3

You work best when your mind is clear, and you are able to focus on your research, thinking and planning. **The key to your mind staying sharp is simple - SLEEP, EAT, EXERCISE & RELAX.** Just repeat each day, week and month!

SLEEP, EAT, EXERCISE & RELAX.

SLEEP, EAT, EXERCISE & RELAX.

SLEEP, EAT, EXERCISE & RELAX.

SLEEP, EAT, EXERCISE & RELAX.

SLEEP, EAT, EXERCISE & RELAX.

SLEEP, EAT, EXERCISE & RELAX.

SLEEP, EAT, EXERCISE & RELAX.

SLEEP, EAT, EXERCISE & RELAX.

Research shows that when you sleep well you can process information more efficiently. You can see the connections and problem solve much better when you are refreshed. Even whilst you are asleep your sub-conscious mind is at work and can problem solve, so it pays to get a good night's sleep. You will also work far more effectively during the day if you are not tired and exhausted by lack of sleep.

A healthy diet with the odd treat makes you far more productive than unhealthy food which tends to make you feel sluggish and tired. Save the unhealthy treats for when you are not actively working on your dissertation, weekends or special occasions!

Exercise is key to staying healthy and getting to the end of your dissertation. Prolonged periods of sitting at a desk can have adverse health implications. Make sure that you take regular breaks, walk around and exercise those busy typing fingers, wrists, arms, shoulders and backs. Try to get out and carry out some sort of more strenuous activities at least three times a week. You choose your activity but get out and enjoy it.

Relax. You cannot work 24/7. Recharge your "batteries" by having some time off to relax and socialise with friends and family. The key to staying motivated and mentally fit for the law dissertation marathon is taking time out to enjoy yourself and relax so that when you go back to your work you feel motivated. Remember this is a long-distance marathon. There will inevitably be stressful periods as you approach your deadline. You will have short periods of intensive work but even in these times you need to take short breaks to relax even if it is just thirty minutes to go for a walk, listen to music or meet a friend for coffee. Allocate time for regular short breaks in your schedule as this will help to pace your work even in the stressful periods.

SURVIVAL TIP 4

There will be stressful times in every project, where you may have doubts or problems. This is a great time to use the support that is available for you at your university. This may be library support, research skills support or support from a designated supervision tutor.

Most students have supervision sessions with a designated tutor at some stage during their law dissertation preparation. Take every advantage of these sessions to work through options and problem issues with an experienced tutor. This means that you must be on top of your preparation, planning and research so you can identify problems or issues that you need guidance on. If you leave everything to the last minute when problems arise it may be too late to get in touch with your tutor or other support services. If you don't have a supervision session planned most tutors are available to offer support and guidance via email or telephone.

Reach out and get the help and support you need. This includes keeping your supervisor appraised of any practical, health or personal problems that affect the preparation of your dissertation. Don't leave problems until an approaching deadline before revealing legitimate problems that you have encountered. You have more time to find solutions with your supervisor the sooner you notify her/him.

Check out a new online platform, my good friend Christine Steel, has just set up to help students contact experts for a professional insight into academic problems.

Mobile Minds online provides academic support when you need it. Connecting students and experts on an online platform. For students studying law, accountancy, actuarial or marketing subjects. Post a Problem at www.mobilemindsonline.com and access help from a qualified expert.

SURVIVAL TIP 5

Just when you think all is going well some students are struck by an intense feeling that their work is not good enough, that they are not as bright as other people think and that their law dissertation will be a failure. These students want their work to be "perfect" and find flaws and errors that don't exist. They want significantly to change or edit perfectly good work. This is the student, who dangerously late in their timetable, wants to change direction, rip-up their work and start again. Worse sometimes they just can't identify the problem but feel nothing is "right" with their work.

This is what is called **"imposter syndrome"**, a psychological feeling of self-doubt, when some students doubt their abilities and accomplishments. This self-doubt is accompanied by a feeling that your perceived lack of ability will be discovered and exposed when you submit your law dissertation.

Don't believe this nagging feeling. You would not have accomplished all you have if you were not a bright, intelligent person with something to contribute to your chosen subject. The last thing you need is unnecessary stress. This is a syndrome to stamp out as soon as it appears. Try to see this problem for what it is: a transitory feeling of doubt.

The best way of dealing with this syndrome is, like any problem, is to acknowledge what it is. Talk to a close friend or family member; they can help put these feeling into context. If the feelings are persistent and begin adversely to affect your work, speak to a university or student counsellor straight away.

SURVIVAL TIP 6

When you have finished writing your dissertation leave it alone for a couple of days [more if you have time] and then go back and re-read it. Edit anything that now appears unclear–those ambiguous phrases, unnecessary words, paragraphs in the wrong places, spelling or grammar errors. Repeat this process at least twice.

You can apply this process to each chapter or to sections of your dissertation as you write. Choose the process that you find easier. Remember that you should aim to read your complete dissertation–the final version at least once. Take yourself somewhere you will not be disturbed and just read as if you had not read it before. This final reading should help you pick up any minor errors with clarity, spelling or grammar. Under no circumstances should you rely totally on the spelling checker and submit your work without carefully reading the final version.

Make sure your appendices are correctly labelled, references correctly cited and that you have included everything you have read and researched in your bibliography. Thank people who have helped and supported your research.

WRITE DISSERTATION

[first draft]

READ

EDIT

CHECK

[SPELLING, GRAMMAR & PROOF READ]

÷

LEAVE FOR A COUPLE OF DAYS/WEEK[S]

[2nd draft]

READ

EDIT

CHECK

[SPELLING, GRAMMAR & PROOF READ]

÷

LEAVE FOR A COUPLE OF DAYS/WEEK[S]

[3rd draft]

READ

EDIT

CHECK

[SPELLING, GRAMMAR & PROOF READ]

÷

LEAVE FOR A WEEK [S]

[final version]

READ

EDIT

CHECK

[SPELLING, GRAMMAR & PROOF READ]

SURVIVAL TIP 7

When you are satisfied with the final version of your law dissertation, print and check that all pages, appendices and the correct version of your dissertation has printed. What a nightmare it would be if you printed the wrong version, left out pages or appendices! Makes sure the dissertation is printed in the correct format required by your university rules.

DISSERTATION DONE DAY!

At the beginning of this process [Survival Tip 1] you sat down and imagined what you were going to do when you submitted your dissertation. You have walked to the school office and handed in your dissertation or submitted it electronically. You have done a great job, your best work and NOW it is time to celebrate...enjoy! You deserve it.

Dissertation Done Day

APPENDIX A

READ. EVALUATE. DECIDE (RED)

I recommend that you use RED–Read Evaluate & Decide. This is a strategy to help you think clearly and logically. If you are a law student, studying for a post-graduate course you will find "10 Reasons You didn't Write an Outstanding Opinion" will help you understand RED when reading and writing legal opinions. The book is available from Amazon.

Learning Styles

If you have read my earlier books you will know that I believe students should read and record information in a style that suits their learning style. When you read and research your law dissertation you will focus and learn more effectively if you use your preferred learning style to record information. Just to recap briefly there are 4 main learning styles–

- VISUAL (seeing) learners.  **"Seeing is believing"** Visual learners remember what they have seen. These learners like colours, pictures and visual infographics or mood-boards to record information.

- READING (read & write) learners. **"I have read"** says the read & write learner. These learners prefer to read information and then write lengthy and detailed notes.

- HEARING (aural) learners. **"I hear you", says the hearing learner.** These learners need to discuss or record information.

- DOING (kinaesthetic) learners. **They learn by doing practical tasks**, building and making things. "I made a model and from that I discovered ..." ... says the **doing learner**. These learners prefer to design, replicate or construct models to help them understand and record information.

You will also find a FREE checklist and PPT slides to help you with your law dissertation to download at www.inspiredtostudy.org You can also book a FREE consultation, to discuss whether you would benefit from your own study coach.

APPENDIX B

Example of completed assessment criteria form

Distinction grade descriptors	Grade Range	Merit/Commendation descriptors	Grade Range	Key words that denote a top dissertation
Exceptional independent research	100-70	Very good research	69-60	Exceptional independent research
Excellent research design		Well researched with significant independent engagement with research		
Demonstrates a rigorous application of methodology and analysis		Thorough methodology		Rigorous methodology & analysis
Innovative & original		Original		Innovative
Detailed understanding of subject/topic		Very good understanding of subject		Detailed understanding of subject
Excellent critical analysis, reflective and thought provoking		Thorough and persuasive		Excellent critical analysis, reflective and thought provoking
Demonstrates exceptional clarity and coherent style		Clearly written and coherent		Exceptional clarity & coherent
Excellent presentation		Extremely well written		Excellent presentation

Appendix C

10 Useful Resources for Research

1. The Bodleian Library-Legal Databases
   https://www.bodleian.ox.ac.uk/law/popular-links/databases

2. The British Library–Law and legal studies
   https://www.bl.uk/subjects/law-and-legal-studies

3. Inner Temple Library Access to Law
   https://www.accesstolaw.com

4. International Research Tutorial
   https://law.duke.edu/ilrt/

5. Middle Temple Library
   https://www.middletemple.org.uk/library-and-archive/library/electronic-resources

6. Ministry of Justice
   https://www.justice.gov.uk/courts/procedure-rules/civil

7. The Law Society Library and online resources -
   https://wv-tls.olib.oclc.org/webview

8. The Open University–Safari to help you improve your digital and information skills
   http://www.open.ac.uk/safari/

9. OSCOLA–Guidance on how to cite legal authorities
   https://www.law.ox.ac.uk/research-subject-groups/publications/oscola

10. CHECK OUT YOUR OWN UNIVERSITY LAW LIBRARY–for training and research sheets to help you with your legal research.

APPENDIX D

The Key to maximising Your MARKS is also four words:

SLEEP.

EAT.

EXERCISE.

RELAX.

There is no point spending hours sitting at a desk if you are not ready or able to study. It is essential that you understand that being healthy is a part of your preparation for effective study. If you are tired, ill or have poor concentration your study will NOT be effective. The solutions - four simple steps:

SLEEP

EAT

EXERCISE

RELAX

THE 'I DON'T HAVE TIME' EXCUSE

You don't have time to eat, sleep, exercise or relax because you have a dissertation to write. Your whole ability to think logically is dependent on these four simple steps. When you are tired and stressed you produce your worst work because your thinking is not clear or logical. Your ability to judge the quality of your work is badly affected by a lack of sleep, lack of exercise, stress and a persistently poor diet.

THE POWER OF SLEEP

Have you heard of the phrase 'I want to sleep on it'? It generally means someone wants more time to think about a decision, usually overnight while they sleep on the problem. Research has shown that whilst sleeping the mind can find solutions and connections that the conscious mind could not make whilst awake[2].

---

[2] Nature 2004 Jan 22, Sleep Inspires insight, by Wagner U, Gais S, Haider H, Verleger R and Born J

Your ability to form arguments, make connections and find solutions to those tough questions could be improved by a good night's sleep.

EAT

You cannot study properly whilst you are hungry, so eat well. You need to keep hydrated so also drink plenty of water. This is not the time to be skipping meals or forgetting to drink during the day. You need energy and water to think and write well. If the brain does not have to worry about food and water, it will be ready and able to focus on research and writing that dissertation.

Do you want some help with easy healthy food recipes? Go to Snig's Kitchen for a celebration of food from around the world, recipes, cooking tips and reviews

http://snigskitchen.blogspot.co.uk/

EXERCISE

You cannot spend all your time at your desk. There are serious health consequences of spending too much time sitting at a desk[3]. Researchers recommend breaking up sitting after 30 minutes with one to two minutes of short activity. Have a look at the recommended fitness guidelines for activity and try some of the fitness exercises[4].

RECENT RESEARCH

Recent research from Stanford University found that walking helped to boost the creative thinking of people undergoing testing compared with those who were seated during the test period. For those in the test, walking outside had even better test results. The research concluded: "Walking opens up the free flow of ideas, and it is a simple and robust solution to the goals of increasing creativity and increasing physical activity."[5] Have a break between classes and lectures, go to the gym, go for a walk with friends or just get some fresh air.

RELAX

We all have periods when stressful events happen, that is life. All colleges and universities have teachers and counsellors who are

---

[3] https://www.nhs.uk/live-well/exercise/why-sitting-too-much-is-bad-for-us/ These range from the risks associated with obesity, diabetes, cardiovascular events and some forms of cancer.

[4] https://www.nhs.uk/live-well/exercise/free-fitness-ideas/ See the recommended activity levels and try some fitness exercises.

[5] Oppezzo, Marily; Schwartz, Daniel L. Journal of Experimental Psychology: Learning, Memory, and Cognition, Vol 40(4), Jul 2014, 1142-1152.

committed to helping you with any personal problems so reach out and get that help. There are wellbeing classes and courses that help you find coping strategies when you feel stressed and help you understand the factors that trigger stress. Remember relaxing also means having fun, so go out and enjoy yourself with friends and family. Take an evening off and do something you enjoy. When you return to your studies you will feel refreshed, ready to focus on your dissertation.

Relax and mediate with the Insight Timer App

https://insighttimer.com

This mediation App has everything you need to relax - thousands of mediations, music and talks in a FREE App. Try to use it daily for at least 28 days and you will appreciate the benefits of mediation and relaxation.

I use this App daily and it has helped to transform my life. I wish you a positive, happy and healthy transformation!

BIBLIOGRAPHY

Fry Ketteridge and Marshall. (2003). *A Handbook for Teaching and Learning in Higher Education*. London: Kogan Page.

Nature 2004 Jan 22, Sleep Inspires insight, by Wagner U, Gais S, Haider H, Verleger R and Born J

NHS Health A-Z. (2017, August 17). *NHS.uk*. Retrieved from https://www.nhs.uk/livewell/exercise/why-sitting-too-much-is-bad-for-us/

NHS Health A-Z. (2017, August 17). *NHS.uk*. Retrieved from https://www.nhs.uk/live-well/exercise/free-fitness-ideas/

Oppezzo, M., & L, S. D. (2014 July). Learning , Memory and Cognition. *Journal of Experimental Psychology vol 40 (4)*, 1142-1152.

About the Author

Suzanne Reece is an education coach. She is a non-practising so-licitor who worked in legal firms for over 17 years. She later moved into education teaching on the Bar Professional Training Course (BPTC) at City, University of London for nearly 10 years.

Suzanne supervised LLM students in their practice focused disser-tations and gained valuable insight on helping students to improve their grades. She taught on the BPTC opinion writing, drafting and civil litigation courses. She co-ordinated and taught civil ad-vocacy. She also has a wealth of experience in designing and mark-ing assessments.

Early in her education career it became apparent that good stu-dents were not achieving the grades they deserved. Suzanne dis-covered with the right coaching students can unlock their poten-tial and qualify in their chosen career.

In 2015, she established Inspired to Study Ltd. A bespoke educational company specialising in skills coaching and mentoring to help post-graduate law students develop their study, work and life skills. Suzanne provides personal coaching and mentoring. She runs regular workshops and attends speaking events. To find our more visit, www.inspiredtostudy.org

Suzanne Reece
The Study Coach
Education Coach, Lecturer & Author

ACKNOWLEDGMENTS

Special thanks to my brother and sister, Arlon and Deborah Reece, for their love.

To my brilliant team of supporters who have helped to edit, check, review and encouraged the birth of this book: To Sian and Hayley for their careful proof reading, checking and editing. To Saddy for her kind words in the Foreword.

To all those who gave helpful suggestions, support and encouragement: Paul Brooks, Hayley Brown, Paula Edwards, George Georgiou, Shirley Harper, Lesley Reece, Sian Lewis, Ian Martin, Deborah Reece, Peter Rosemin, Surinder Tamne, Gillian Woodworth. Special thanks to Ella Brown my adopted god-daughter and the next super-hero.

A special thanks to ALL my former BPTC law students at City, University of London for the privilege of sharing their many achievements.

Internal formatting and arrangement by Chad Robertson www.writingnights.org

Book covers designed by Vanessa Mendozzi, Graphic designer www.vanessamendozzidesign.com

Made in the USA
Coppell, TX
24 March 2022

75450631R00066